Les,

Enj o

Mike

Line by Line

Forensic Document Examination

A Strategy for Legal Professionals

Michael Wakshull

Line by Line – Forensic Document Examination – A Strategy for Legal Professionals

Copyright © 2013 Michael Wakshull
       www.Q9Consulting.com
       MikeW@Quality9.com

Cover and Interior Design by Steven W. Booth,
       www.GeniusBookServices.com

ISBN: 978-0-9857294-0-0

Contents

Figures

Dedicated to my wife Jan and the many teachers who have unselfishly shared their wealth of knowledge.

Introduction

Line by Line — Forensic Document Examination — A Strategy for Legal Professionals

provides an overview of forensic document examination that will enable attorneys and other legal professionals to better prepare for criminal and civil trials. It dispels possible misunderstandings about the work a forensic document examiner performs and how a document examiner reaches conclusions. This in-depth guide is designed to help attorneys and other legal professionals avoid the pitfalls that can sometimes occur when using forensic document examination to determine the authenticity of handwriting and documents.

You are likely reading this book because you have had cases requiring a forensic document examiner or expect to have a case requiring a forensic document examiner. ***Line by Line — Forensic Document Examination — A Strategy for Legal Professionals*** offers legal practitioners insight into the work of forensic document examiners. It provides a guide to types of cases document examiners investigate, how attorneys can partner with a document examiner to develop the theme of the case and deliverables to expect from the document examiner.

The audiences for this book are attorneys and others who need to hire a person sufficiently educated and trained in the science of forensic document examination. The term "expert" is intentionally omitted from the description of the document examiner. Only a court can designate a person as an expert.

Many famous cases in the last century have turned on the results of handwriting identification, including The Lindbergh baby kidnapping, Mormon will, Howard Hughes diary, Hitler diaries, Salamander letter and many others. Handwriting has been examined to solve, unsuccessfully, the Jonbenet Ramsey murder and many other cases. In many of these and other cases, document examiners' analyses resulted in divergent opinions about whether someone wrote the document. Cases such as Clifford Irving's Howard Hughes autobiography and Mark Hofmann's Salamander letter have fooled experienced document examiners who opined they were authentic when they were forgeries

Often prospective clients report to the document examiner a case is straightforward. The trained document examiner may determine a case is more complex than was determined by the untrained layperson. When reading this book, the layperson can obtain knowledge about the difficulties a document examiner experiences while reaching an opinion.

Document examiners are hired researchers. They advocate for neither side in a dispute. Their sole allegiance is to the evidence. Document examiners who are members of professional organizations, such as the National Association of Document Examiners or American Society of Questioned Document Examiners, subscribe to a code of ethics which prohibits improperly supporting the desired outcome of any party, including the party who hired the document examiner.

When the document examiner must report other conclusions than the party's desired outcome, this aids the attorney by showing the client may not have a valid case. In one instance, an attorney wanted to retain my services for a case where his client stated he did not sign a contract. Exemplar documents were not forthcoming. The client later admitted in a deposition to having signed the document. We did not go forward with the case.

Document examiners express their conclusions as opinions rather than fact. The reason is explained later. Document examiners do not prove a statement.

Black's Law Dictionary Ninth Edition (Garner, 2009) defines *forensic* as, "Used in suitable courts of law or public debate." Forensic document examination means authenticating documents for the legal community when a question arises about a document. The question may be:

- "Who wrote the document?"

- "Who signed the document?"

- "Did someone alter a document?"

- "On what printer was the document print-ed?"

- "Is the stamp produced by ink or on a printer with toner?

- "Was the signature added to the document with software?"

- Many other possible questions may be asked.

The majority of work performed by document examiners involves analysis of handwriting. Much of the handwriting examination work is determination of the authenticity of signatures. The document examiner is asked to determine who signed a document or whether a specific person signed a document.

Besides signatures, document examiners review handwritten text on a document. In one case, I was given several pages of questioned writing and several pages of writing known to have been written by three people. The question was whether one or more of the writers of the known writing had written the questioned text. The result of the analysis was one of the writers of the known writing did write the questioned writing.

Document examiners may determine whether documents were printed on the same printer. In these cases, a microscope may be used to examine the way the letters are formed on the page and the type of printer that created the characters on the page. Document examiners look at the way the pages were printed, such as whether they were printed on a laser printer, ink jet printer, wax printer, or other type of printer. Two documents may look the same to our eyes, but when examining them under a microscope the type of printer used to create the document becomes apparent.

What is Forensic Document Examination?

Black's Law Dictionary defines a ***document*** as, 1) "Something tangible on which words, symbols or marks are recorded," and 2) "The deeds, agreements, title papers, letters, receipts, and other written instruments used to prove a fact." In today's environment, documents are also intangible, computer generated images, such as a scan of a tangible item, an e-mail, a signature written on a digital pad, a photograph or a report written on a computer. Document examiners must have the skills necessary to examine all of these documents.

According to the Scientific Working Group for Forensic Document Examination (www.swgdoc.org), "The forensic document examiner conducts scientific examinations, comparisons, and analyses of documents in order to: (1) establish genuineness or non-genuineness, or to reveal alterations, additions, or deletions, (2) identify or eliminate persons as the source of handwriting, (3) identify or eliminate the source of machine produced documents, typewriting, or other impression marks, or relative evidence, and (4) preserve and/or restore legibility. They also write technical reports and give expert testimony."

Written documents are not always on common writing materials. They may be graffiti written on walls. Some documents are created with mechanical printers, such as an ink jet or toner laser printers and photocopy machines. A document examiner needs to be able to distinguish among different forms of mechanical printing.

When a document is written on paper, the document includes the paper, ink by which the words were written, the toner or ink used by the mechanical printer and any other marks on the page. All these can offer clues to the authenticity of a document.

When authenticating handwriting, document examiners need many samples of the suspected writer's writing. The samples are called "exemplars." In many cases, 20 or more samples of a person's writing are needed.

Document examiners must use a scientifically based approach to authenticate documents. Failure to use a scientifically based approach to their work may cause the court disallow the testimony. Document examiners must be ready to testify about their opinion in a legal proceeding, such as a deposition, arbitration or trial. Their opinions must be substantiated with valid reasons and approaches to their work methodology. If a document examiner walks into a courtroom and says, "I believe this document was written by the same person," or "The person you think wrote it did not write it," because that is my opinion, that does not go very far. The method for reaching an opinion must be verifiable and repeatable.

A scientific approach means the document examiner starts with a hypothesis and tries to disprove the hypothesis. A hypothesis is an assumption you want to test in order to determine its validity. This means an examiner may start with a hypothesis that two documents were written by the same person. As an analyst and scientist, the examiner looks at the documents and asks, "Can I show they were not written by the same person?" If there is a way the examiner can say, "These were not written by the same person," the examiner would opine they are not written by the same person. If the examiner cannot show the documents were not written by the same person, then the examiner may say they were written by the same person. Alternatively, if the evidence does not demonstrate the document was absolutely written by the same person or not written by the same person, the examiner may give a qualified opinion which leaves room for doubt or state "no conclusion." Document examiners cannot prove a hypothesis. They can only accept the hypothesis as true and leave the door open that it is not true.

Document examiners refer to handwriting as brain writing. Handwriting is a psychomotor interaction where the brain tells the muscles how to work the arm and hand in order to write. The pen is not executing the writing. It is the whole body that is executing the writing.

Authentication of Documents

Black's Law Dictionary (Garner, 2009) defines authenticate as, 1) "To prove the genuineness of (a thing)" and 2. "To render authoritative or authentic, as by attestation or other legal formality."

Document examiners offer evidence to support an opinion. The opinion is a result of examination of all information that has been provided. The document examiner may request additional information from a client because the evidence provided is insufficient to form an opinion in any direction.

The opinion may be conclusive at an extreme or fall in the middle as inconclusive. A conclusive opinion of "identify" means the document examiner believes, based on all provided evidence, the author of the known writing wrote the questioned document. A conclusive opinion of "eliminate" means the evidence is clear the author of the known writing did not write the questioned document.

Even a conclusive opinion leaves the door open for being revised should additional evidence surface.

Other forms of authentication may be determining whether a document has been altered. Examples of alteration include:

- Changing letters or numbers such as changing a 1 to a 7 or a 4 to a 9 in order to collect a larger sum of money or changing the date on a document.

- After having made an error in a procedure, a person may attempt to cover his error by adding language to a report.

- A page of a contract may be retyped to modify terms then printed on and inserted into the set of pages hoping no one will discover the change.

- A bank check may be chemically washed to remove the payee and amount so a new payee and amount can be inserted.

- Insertion of text in a record

Chapter 1 – Laws and Standards for Document Examination

Document examiners must understand the law pertaining to providing expert testimony. In 1923, Frye v. United States, 293 F. 1013 (D.C. Cir. *1923*), developed law as to the admissibility of expert testimony. The Frye case establishes that experts must use generally accepted practices in the industry when performing examinations. The 1993, Daubert v. Merrell Dow Pharmaceuticals (92-102), 509 U.S. 579 (1993) changed the requirements for expert testimony in federal court in Rule 702 of the Federal Rules of Evidence. Many states have adopted the Daubert approach, which makes the judge the gatekeeper who decides whether an expert is permitted to testify. The intent is to keep "junk science" out of the courtroom. Daubert established a test establishing the validity of the methodology used:

1. Empirical testing: The theory or technique must be falsifiable, refutable, and testable.

2. Subjected to peer review and publication.

3. Known or potential error rate.

4. The existence and maintenance of standards

and controls concerning its operation.

5. Degree to which the theory and technique is generally accepted by a relevant scientific community.

In United States v. Starzecpyzel, 93 Cr 553 (LMM), 880 Fed. Sup. 1027 (S Dist N.Y. 1995), the court determined document examiners are "skilled experts" rather than scientists. Following Daubert, Kumho Tire Co. v. Carmichael, 526 U.S. 137 (1999) applied the Daubert standard to all expert testimony, not just testimony from scientists. Therefore, the Daubert tests apply to forensic document examiners.

Standards for Forensic Document Examiners

There are 19 standards used by document examiners. The standards are developed by ASTM International. Section E30 of ASTM is forensics. Section E30.02 was for forensic document examination. In February 2012, committee E30.02 was disbanded. The document examination standards were moved to committee E30.90.

Standard E1658 defines the nine-point scale used by document examiners to express their opinions. Standard E2388 defines the minimal education requirements for document examiners. The standards define a base methodology for examination of documents. La Trobe University in Melbourne, Australia published an 11-step procedure for examination of handwritten documents. The methodology is well tested and validated. If a document examiner follows the ASTM or La Trobe methodology, the document examiner is following a generally accepted practice for the discipline.

The ASTM Standards are:

Standard	Title of Standard
E444	Scope of Work for Forensic Document Examiners
E1422	Standard Guide for Test Methods for Forensic Writing Ink Comparison
E1658	Standard Terminology for Expressing Conclusions for Forensic Document Examiners
E1789	Standard Guide for Writing Ink Comparison
E2195	Standard Terminology Relating to the Examination of Questioned Documents
E2285	Standard Guide for Examination of Mechanical Checkwriter Impressions
E2286	Standard Guide for Examination of Dry Seal Impressions
E2287	Standard Guide for Examination of Fracture Patterns and Paper Fiber Impressions on Single-Strike Film Ribbons for Typed Text
E2288	Standard Guide for Physical Match of Paper Cuts, Tears and Perforations in Forensic Document Examination
E2289	Standard Guide for Examination of Rubber Stamp Impressions
E2290	Standard Guide for Examination of Handwritten Items
E2291	Standard Guide for Indentation Examinations
E2325	Standard Guide for Non-Destructive Examination of Paper
E2331	Standard Guide for Examination of Altered Documents
E2388	Standard Guide for Minimum Training Requirements for Forensic Document Examiners
E2389	Standard Guide for Examination of Documents Produced With Liquid Ink Jet Technology
E2390	Standard Guide for Examination of Documents Produced With Toner Technology
E2494	Standard Guide for Examination of Typewritten Items
E2765	Standard Practice for Use of Image Capture and Storage Technology in Forensic Document Examination

Huber & Hedrick (1999) proposed 21 elements for discrimination of handwriting.

1. Arrangement

2. Class of allograph (cursive, manuscript, printing, composite)

3. Connections (interword and intraword)

4. Designs of allographs and their construction

5. Dimensions

6. Slant and slope

7. Spacings (interword and intraword)

8. Abbreviations

9. Alignment

10. Commencements and terminations

11. Diacritics and punctuations (presence, style and location)

12. Embellishments

13. Legibility or writing quality

14. Line continuity

15. Line quality

16. Pen control

17. Writing movement

18. Consistency or natural variation

19. Persistency

20. Lateral Expansion

21. Word proportions

Document Examiners' Opinions

Document examiners' opinions are expressed in qualified or unqualified form per ASTM standard E1658, which states nine levels of opinion. The unqualified opinions are: 1) identification and 2) elimination. The middle of the scale is "No conclusion." The qualified opinions are: indications, probably, and strong probability in each direction from the center.

Opinion Scale for Forensic Document Examiners – ASTM E1658-04

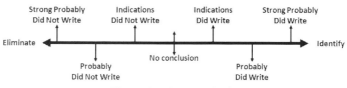

Figure 1 – Opinion Scale

Identify means the document examiner is convinced the writer of the known writing is the writer of the questioned writing. Elimination means the document examiner is convinced the writer of the known writing is not the writer of the questioned writing. This applies to determination of the authenticity of a document. As an example, identification means the document examiner is convinced the document is authentic.

Document examiners must be careful when giving an unqualified opinion. The opinions affect people's lives. For this reason, authorities state we need a sufficient number of exemplars to perform the examination of writing or documents. Determination of variability of the writing requires enough exemplars to know how a person writes. There is no specific number of exemplars needed. The answer to how many are needed is, "a sufficient number to draw a valid conclusion." The document examiner's responsibility is to continue requesting additional exemplars until a valid opinion can be reached. Otherwise, an inconclusive opinion may be the correct opinion.

An initially qualified opinion may result when the data is not sufficient to resolve all differences between the known writing and the questioned writing. When this occurs, the document examiner asks the client to look for additional exemplars to resolve the differences. Too many exemplars are better than too few. Providing too few exemplars increases the cost of the examination since the document examiner must stop then restart the analysis when additional exemplars are delivered. When measuring to determine the variability of the writing, at least 12 exemplars are needed. Additional exemplars strengthen the assessment of the variability.

When the opinion is toward identification, fewer samples may be needed than if the opinion is toward elimination. The reason for identification is the writing may be so similar the chance of two people having written the documents is very small. Elimination requires enough samples to determine whether features in the questioned writing appear in the known writing. At a trial to determine the authenticity of a holographic will the opposing examiner had two exemplars. Based on the two exemplars, the opposing examiner opined the decedent had not authored the will. I had more than 20 exemplars. Because I had so many exemplars, I was able to show features of the questioned writing the opposing examiner stated did not appear in the known writing. My opinion was there is a strong probability the decedent wrote the will. The court agreed with my opinion.

Chapter 2 – Document Examiners' Tools

A digital microscope can be used to capture an enlarged image onto a computer. An example of a high end digital microscope is called MiScope from Zarbeco in New Jersey. The microscope has many built-in capabilities, such as variable magnification, software to capture the image, built-in infrared and ultraviolet light lamps etc.

An optical stereo microscope provides a magnified three-dimensional look at an image. A trinocular version permits attaching a camera onto the third tube on top in order to photograph the image seen through the eyepieces. When a digital camera is attached, the image can be sent directly to the computer. The digital camera is the small black box on top of the trinocular tube. The wire is the connector to the computer.

Infrared and Ultraviolet viewing scopes, such as a Find–R–Scope, allow looking at a document with alternative light sources that are outside the visibility of the human eye. Filters of different wavelengths may be attached to the viewing scopes to see the document differently. These are often used to determine whether a document has been altered.

A Lupe is a small magnifier user to examine a portion of a document. The image is not typically photographed through a lupe. Lupes come in various magnification levels, such as 10x, 15x, 20x.

A NIST (National Institute for Standards and Technology) *Standard Ruler* is a specially calibrated metal

ruler. The ruler has increments small as 1/100 inch. The examiner places the ruler under a lupe or micro-

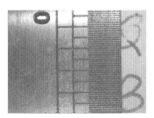

scope in order to read the length being measured. The NIST standard ruler is precise at 68 degrees Fahrenheit (20 degrees Celsius). The bottom image is a magnification of a ruler adjacent to letters which are to be measured.

Adobe Photoshop™ *software* is a powerful tool used by document examiners to compare writing, determine alterations, examine digital images and many other functions. Photoshop allows a document examiner to cut a section of writing on one document and overlay it onto a similar writing on another document. This is valuable when determining whether a character or set of characters in the questioned writing is similar to the same set of characters in known writing. Photoshop is used for examination of ink and enhancement of images.

A Computer is used to store all digital images, write reports, create demonstrative exhibits etc. A laptop computer enables the document examiner to examine documents outside the document examiner's laboratory. The portable digital microscope, flatbed scanner and other equipment can be attached to capture the images of the documents directly to the computer for examination.

A Flatbed scanner is used to scan documents into the computer. Once the documents are stored in the

computer, they can be examined using Photoshop. This allows the examiner to work with the document without concern of harming the source document. A flatbed scanner is used rather than a sheet-fed scanner. A sheet-fed scanner uses wheels to pull the document across the scanning device. The wheels can potentially mark or damage the document. In a flatbed scanner, the document is placed onto glass without any moving parts touching the document.

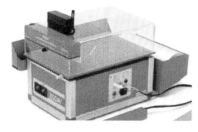

Electrostatic detection device is used to detect indented writing. The device shown here is an ESDA, manufactured by Foster and Freeman from England. Indented writing is writing that appears on a page below the page on which a person writes on a pad or stack of paper. The indented writing is an impression caused by the pressure of the pen on the page above, which tells the document examiner what was written on the page above. The electrostatic detection device can show impressions of what was written on several pages above. This device can be used to assist with solving the problem of which line was drawn first.

The video spectral comparator (VSC) is manufactured by Foster and Freeman and is expensive. The VSC uses infrared and ultraviolet light to examine a document. VSCs are useful to help solve the line crossing problem and differentiation of inks

Hyperspectral imaging system Video Spectral Comparator HSI Examiner™ 100 QD. The HIS is manufactured by ChemImage from Pittsburgh, Pennsylvania. The HSI Examiner™ is typically used by government laboratories for authentication of government documents such as passports, driver's licenses etc. The HSI Examiner price starts around $90,000 USD.

Digital calipers (example is manufactured by Mitutoyo) are used to measure the thickness of paper. This is valuable when the document examiner needs to determine whether a page in a document may have been taken from a different ream than the rest of the pages in a document.

The document examiner uses *gloves* when handling original documents. Human hands have oils which can contaminate documents. This is especially true if the document is to be examined for fingerprints. The document examiner does not want to add his/her fingerprints to the document. Nitrile gloves are the best type of gloves since the nitrile does not pass oils through the material.

Chapter 3 – Each Assignment is a Unique Research Project

T.S. Eliot (1943) wrote, "We shall not cease from exploration and the end of all our exploring will be to arrive where we started and know the place for the first time." Document examiners are explorers. Every time a document examiner works on a case, it is completely new. Often when a case is received, a client will describe the case as "a slam dunk." To the layperson, the answer whether a person wrote a document often appears obvious. To the trained document examiner, it is not necessarily obvious. As a researcher, the document examiner will sometimes work on a case and then put it aside for a while before returning to the case with a fresh perspective.

I had a case where the client attorney said the case would be simple. The first time I gave an opinion to him, the opinion was, "inconclusive." The exemplars he had given to me were insufficient to determine whether the decedent had executed the signature. Additional exemplars were needed to solve the case. He provided many more samples of the decedent's writing. When additional data was provided, the research eventually yielded an opinion in the case. This turned out to be a complex case. Document examiners cannot say, "I've seen this before so I know the answer."

It's never that way. Each case is a unique project.

Mathematics and probability theory give us additional basis on which to substantiate an opinion. The basis of handwriting identification is for the document examiner to understand the variability of a person's writing. Variability is a mathematical concept. By applying the mathematics of variability to the handwriting, a document examiner is better able to obtain indications about how to proceed with the research. The result determines whether the questioned writing may have come from the same set of writing as the known writing.

Dr. Sargur Srihari at the State University of New York at Buffalo stated we must develop a scientific basis that is based on error rates. Srihari lead a team to develop computer software for the United States Post Office for handwriting identification based on a statistical approach. The software uses digital image processing and pattern recognition for identification of writers. Based upon Srihari's work, much additional research has been conducted to identify writers using statistically based analysis.

The International Graphonomics Society and the Institute of Electrical and Electronic Engineers (IEEE) Special Interest Group on Pattern Recognition publish a substantial amount of research using computers and statistical analysis for writer identification.

Chapter 4 – Document Examination Procedures

Types of Exemplars

Document examiners must compare known writing forms with the questioned document. Writing can be printed, manuscript, cursive, or mixed print and cursive. Signatures are needed to compare with a questioned signature. Standard writing is compared with standard writing. When comparing writing, the source writing is best when it is the same type of writing as the questioned writing. Normal course of business writing such as a check, contract or other legal document is needed to compare with writing on a legal document. A letter or card to a friend or family requires other informal writing. We tend to write differently, especially a signature, in different circumstances. At a presentation by neurologist Dr. Evelyne Pannetier at the 2011 National Association of Document Examiners conference in Montreal, Dr. Pannetier described how we write differently depending whether we are writing freely, taking dictation or copying. The reason is different parts of the brain are involved in the neuromotor coordination. When taking request exemplars, the document examiner requests many iterations of writing so the subject becomes more fluid in writing. The writing becomes more natural than the first iterations.

Request Exemplars

When an insufficient number of exemplars are available to perform an examination, the suspect may be asked to provide examples of writing. The writing may be a series of signatures, the text that is in question or text that represents words and characters in the questioned writing.

It is important to work with the document examiner to prepare and take the request exemplars. Your case may be compromised if the request exemplars are taken incorrectly. Incorrect request exemplars may result in writing that is not representative of the needed writing.

In one case, I recommended to the attorney we demand request exemplars from the suspect because the opposing side was uncooperative in providing examples of the suspect's writing. The retaining attorney submitted a motion to the court for the request exemplars. The motion contained text of a paragraph the suspect would write once. The attorney did not consult with me about the procedure for taking request exemplars. At the writing session, we obtained one sample from the suspect. The written text was of no value. We had one signature for comparison. As a result, a qualified opinion was reached.

Work with the document examiner when request exemplars are required. The document examiner will provide guidance for taking the exemplars. In the last example, the attorney needed to include a request for the suspect to sign and initial duplicate copies of the contract on which the questioned signatures and initials appeared.

The writer should be placed in a setting that emulates the environment in which the questioned writing was written. In another case, the suspect wrote his signature more than 30 times on the same page while sitting at a desk in a lighted room. The questioned signature was written late at night in a car on a dark road on a citation pad. As a result, the request exemplars differed from the questioned signature, and a qualified opinion was rendered. The attorney failed to engage a document examiner when taking the request exemplars.

Examination of Handwriting

Document examiners use two sets of documents for handwriting identification. The known documents are those known to have been written by the person whose writing is being compared with the questioned document. The questioned document is the document on which the examiner will opine as to its authenticity. The more known documents obtained by the document examiner, the stronger the opinion. A document examiner looks at how a person writes because there is variability in the way each person writes. A document examiner must define this variability to determine whether the questioned writing lies within the variability of the known writing.

There is a theory that no two people write exactly the same. This theory is open to controversy. The class of potential writers must be limited to the class of people who potentially could have written the questioned document rather than the population of all people. There are more than 300 million people in the United States. It is nearly impossible to test the theory that no two of these people write in the same manner. How do we know that no two of the 300 million people write the same way?

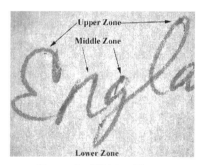

Figure 2 - Writing Zones

Handwriting in the Latin-based alphabets is divided into three zones shown in figure 2. The middle zone is the area in which most lower case letters are written. These are letters such as a, e, r, s etc. The upper zone is the area above the middle zone letters. The top of capital letters and some lower case letters such as b, d, f etc. extend into the upper zone. The lower zone is the area below the baseline or bottom of the middle zone letters. The bottom of lower-case letters, such as g, y, f etc., extend into the lower zone.

Figure 3 - Inter-writer Variability

Inter-writer variability is the way writing varies across different writers. In Figure 3, we see the way four different writers construct the lower case cursive letter "y". Although three of the writers use a stick formation for the lower zone, they are all written very differently. The upper left example slopes down to the right, the upper right is close to vertical while the lower left slopes down to the left. The examples on the left are made with a single stroke, whereas the upper right example is constructed with two strokes. The lower right example places a loop in the lower zone on the loop at the bottom of the "y".

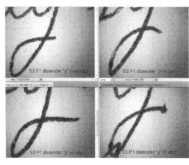

Figure 4 - Intra-writer Variability

Intra-writer variability is the way a single person varies the writing from session to session. Figure 4 shows the distender differs in each of these examples which were written by the same person at different times. Each was written using the same pen. Note that each example has an ink goop in the same location on the upstroke at the bottom of the "y". The upper left example has a wider loop than the other three. The terminus of the stroke in the lower right makes a small loop with an up-stroke that does not exist in the other examples. The length of the horizontal terminal stroke in the bottom left is longer than the other three examples. All examples were written on the same day with a minimum of 15 minutes between writings in order to avoid exact replication of the writings. The same text was written each time. Each example is from a different word in the sentence.

Document examiners need to study the known writing to determine the Intra-writer variability of the known writer. Then they need to determine whether the questioned writing fits within that intra-writer variability.

Figure 5 - Habits in Writing

Ordway Hilton stated, "Habits may be retained that persist across natural evolution of a signature during a person's lifetime. (Hilton, 1992)" Figure 5 includes samples of my writing from 1979 through 2009. One item to notice is the little mark, or goop, in the upstroke of the lower loop of lower-case letters. This always appears regardless of writing instrument or posture when writing. A basic theory of handwriting is there is a consistency in a person's writing. A person is incapable of changing these attributes of writing. Writing is a habit. As we develop graphic maturity, we develop habits that identify the writing as ours regardless of writing instrument used. This can be another clue to identify the writer. Because writing is a habit, it is not just the big structures we make in a similar manner, but we also make the microstructures similarly. These goops are a result of neuromuscular interaction I cannot control. The goops are unique to ball point pens.

Types of Variation

Common cause variation, also called natural variation, is the variability in writing that just happens. This is the intra-writer variability. This variability is explainable. Examples of the cause of common cause variability in handwriting are change of posture, different writing instrument, fatigue of the writer, the purpose of the writing, aging of the writer, illness etc.

Special cause variation is any factor that can be detected and identified as contributing to a change in a quality characteristic or process level. This is not explainable or attributable to the writer. Examples may be a rough line caused by a rough writing surface or a sudden jump caused when the writer was startled. When these appear in the known writing, the examples are disregarded for the analysis. An unexplained anomaly in a questioned writing may be the result of special cause variability.

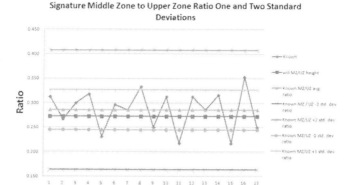

Figure 6 - Natural Variation of Ratios

When applying the scientific method, the common cause (natural) variability can be measured mathematically and shown on a plot. This reduces subjective bias from the analysis. The numbers do not lie or mislead.

The purpose of the chart in Figure 6 is to determine whether the questioned writing falls within the range of the way the known writer writes, or intra-writer variability.

The chart represents the results of measuring the ratio of the height of the upper zone divided by the height of the middle zone. The height of the upper zone is determined by measuring the height of the tallest letter in the signature. The height of the middle zone is determined by measuring the height of the tallest letter in the middle zone. The height of the upper zone is divided by the height of the middle zone to obtain the ratio or proportion as stated in criterion 21 of Huber and Hedrick's 21 criteria. The wavy line represents the ratio of the upper zone to the middle zone in each known signature. This shows the ratio varies for each known signature. This is the intra-writer variability of the known writer. It is the way the writer changes the relative heights of the upper zone and middle zone of his name each time he writes.

The straight line with the squares represents the ratio of the upper zone to the middle zone in the questioned writing. The chart shows the ratio in the signature of the questioned writing lies within the ratios of the known writing. As a result, the document examiner has empirical evidence the writer of the questioned writing may be the writer of the known writing.

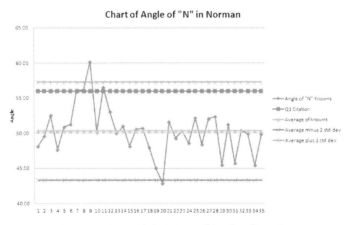

Figure 7 - Natural Variation of Angle of Writing

This is one piece of evidence. It does not mean the writer of the known writing is the writer of the questioned writing. A good simulator may be able to write a signature that falls within the statistical attributes of the known writing.

To apply this test, the document examiner takes several measurements of the known and questioned writing. These measurements may include the angle of writing or spacing between words. These measurements add to the evidence.

Although the attributes of one measurement of the questioned writing may align with the known writing, it is unlikely the attributes of several measurements will align with the known writing when the writing is simulated.

It is possible that even though the person appears to have written the questioned signature, another person may have similar variability in their writing.

Document examiners must determine the cause of the difference between the writings to determine whether a person did or did not write a document or signature. They need to understand possible illusions in writing caused by extraneous marks on a page, such as machine printed writing, drawings, color of paper or other distractions that may cause a writing to look different from another when it may have the same attributes.

In Figure 7, the line that moves up and down represents the measurements of the known writing. The line shows the intra-writer variation. Each number at the bottom of the chart represents a known writing sample. There were 35 known signatures. The dot at the angle represents the angle of a stroke in the relevant stroke in the word "Norman." For sample 1, the angle was approximately 47 degrees. The angle for sample 2 was approximately 48 degrees. The angle for sample 3 was approximately 52 degrees. The horizontal line toward the top with the square box markers represents the angle for the word "Norman" in the questioned document. The line in the center shows the average of the angles for the known writing samples. The top horizontal line is +2 standard deviations from the average of the angle in the known writing. The bottom horizontal line is -2 standard deviations from the average of the angle in the known writing. In this example, the questioned writing falls within a statistically defined intra-writer variability. Therefore, the writer is a valid suspect for having written the questioned writing. The implication is we need to continue with the examination using other generally accepted methods for handwriting identification. A scientific approach is used in this example which demonstrates criterion 6 of Huber and Hedrick's 21 criteria.

Application of measurement and mathematics to writer identification is not new. The ASTM standards encourage knowledge of mathematics for the forensic document examiner. ASTM standard E444, Standard Guide for the Scope of Work of Forensic Document Examiners, states that education from fields such as "… physical sciences, mathematics …" are important for the forensic document examiner.

In 1914, Frank Freeman wrote about measurement

of speed and angles of writing (Freeman, 1914). Freeman stated on page 144 the data was not sufficient for application at that time. In 1929, Robert Saudek expanded on Freeman's work when he published measurement results in *Experiments in Handwriting*. Later, Albert Osborn, Wilson Harrison, Ordway Hilton and others wrote about application of proportion of writing zones to assist identification of a writer. Huber and Hedrick applied the concept of the likelihood ratio to writer identification.

Simulation

Document examiners do not use the word "forge" since forgery implies intent and mental condition. It is a legal term for a trier of fact to determine. A document examiner will only opine that a document is genuine or not genuine. Document examiners use the term "simulation" to state another person copied the writing of another person

Freehand simulation occurs when a person makes no attempt to create an exact copy of the writing of another person. This may be done when the simulator believes the recipient of the writing does not know the writing of the person whose writing is being simulated or the recipient will not verify the writing. Simulation is also accomplished by copying a known signature or writing form or tracing a known signature or writing.

When a document examiner needs to determine whether a specific person simulated a signature, it is valuable for the examiner to obtain the regular writing of suspect, as well as sample signatures. When a person simulates the signature of another person, the result is not a signature, rather it is a drawing of a signature. Signatures often differ in form and appearance from regular course-of-business writing by the same person.

Figure 9 - Simulation

In a case involving a person simulating the signature of another person (Figure 8), I had examples of the suspected simulator's signature and regular writing. In this case, the simulator and the person whose name was simulated shared the letter "S" as the first letter of the first name. When the signature of the simulator was compared with the signature he simulated, the first letters of the name did not match. When the letter "S" was extracted from course-of-business writing and was compared with the first let-

Figure 9 - Simulation

ter of the simulated signature, they matched. As an example, the person's name was Simon. The "S" in Simon was compared with the "S" in "Same."

Figure 9 is another case a person simulated the name "Stella." Her "St" from normal course-of-business writing matched the "St" where she wrote "Stella." The lighter writing is the questioned writing. The black writing is the known writing. When the questioned writing was placed on top of the known writing, the similarities were apparent.

In each case, the person was not able to change his or her standard writing style when attempting to simulate the signature of another person. A simulated signature is a drawing of a signature rather than a true signature. The result is the simulated signature is a variation of the writer's everyday writing

Note
Written in both directions
Only a few words apart

Figure 10 - Writing Direction

Authorities in document examination state people tend to write in a specific manner to construct strokes. They will move in a clockwise or counterclockwise direction each time the same letter is formed. I had a case that dispelled this idea and showed that document examiners need to collect as much evidence as possible. We need to be vigilant about all writing in a document.

In the example in Figure 10, the known document was written using printing style. Upon examining the writing, I noticed the writer constructed the lower-case "a" in an interesting manner. Two lines apart, the base of the "a" was constructed in both a counter-clockwise manner and a clockwise manner. The result was I could not use the directional construction for comparison with the writing of the questioned document. The questioned document showed the writer constructing the lower case "a" in a clockwise direction. Had I only noted the known counter-clockwise "a", an incorrect opinion may have been reached.

Disguised Writing

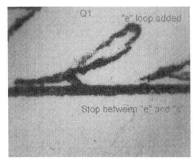

Figure 11 - Disguised Writing

Disguised writing is also known as auto-simulation. A person intentionally disguises a signature or other writing with the intention of disavowing having executed the writing. The purpose may be to later deny having signed a contract or other document. In Figure 11, the person denied having executed a contract for the purpose of not making the required payments. The signature appeared generally fluid when examined with the naked eye. When the signature was examined under a microscope, the patch stroke which was added to disguise the letter "e" was apparent. In the known exemplars, the writer wrote the lower case "e" as a single retraced stroke. He always stopped writing after the "e" leaving a gap before starting the next letter in his name. The gap is apparent in the disguised signature. The attempt at disguising his signature failed when the strokes were magnified.

Infirmity

Figure 12 - Writing of
Infirm Person

The document examiner needs to learn whether the writer of the known documents has an illness or other infirmity which can affect the writing. Diseases of the central nervous system, muscles, pulmonary system or cardiovascular system can induce changes in writing. When infirmity is present the document examiner will request writing exemplars from the time of the questioned writing in order to show writing that either includes or excludes the infirmity.

If the person is infirm, the analysis may be more complex than when the person has no infirmity. The example in Figure 12 shows the tremor induced by illness in an elderly person. This was a known signature from the person whose writing was compared with a questioned signature. In this case, the questioned signature showed little tremor and better speed.

Verification of Exemplars

Figure 13 - Variation of Valid Signatures

A question may arise as to the authenticity of exemplars. Figure 13 is a situation where an attorney gave me a signature on a hospital intake form as an exemplar (image on right). The initial letter "A" of the signature was different from all other exemplars for the subject. It was in the form of a printed "A". The "A" was cursive form in all the other exemplars (image on left) which spanned 50 years. I pointed this out and questioned the authenticity of the exemplar. At my request, the attorney told his client additional exemplars of this format were needed for this to be accepted as an authentic exemplar. Another similar print-style exemplar was produced. The additional exemplar was stipulated as authentic by the party on the other side. Therefore, I accepted the exemplar as demonstrating the subject had two distinct methods of writing the first letter of his name. Note the forward slant of the "A" in both forms is similar.

The document examiner has a duty to question any

exemplar's authenticity. We know as a person ages or becomes infirm, there are often changes to the writing. We must ask questions. There have been cases where a person has tremulous writing at one time and smooth writing shortly thereafter due to drugs which quell the cause of tremor. The document examiner must ask whether the subject is taking medication that quells the tremor before rejecting the exemplars as being legitimate.

Cut and Paste

Cut and paste is done by cutting a known signature or other writing from a document and placing it onto another document then making a copy of the manufactured document. The copy is claimed to be a photocopy of the original document.

Since no one writes exactly the same way twice, if a signature shows an exact match when superimposed onto another signature, the document examiner can be certain either one is a cut and paste of the other. If they are both copies, they may both be cut and paste copies of a third signature.

Using computer software such as Adobe Photoshop™, cut and paste documents appear realistic.

When only copies are available there is no means to determine whether a document is authentic. The signature may be authentic yet it is superimposed onto the document by cut-and-paste techniques. For this reason, always ask your client for the original document. The original can be examined to determine whether it is authentic or fabricated.

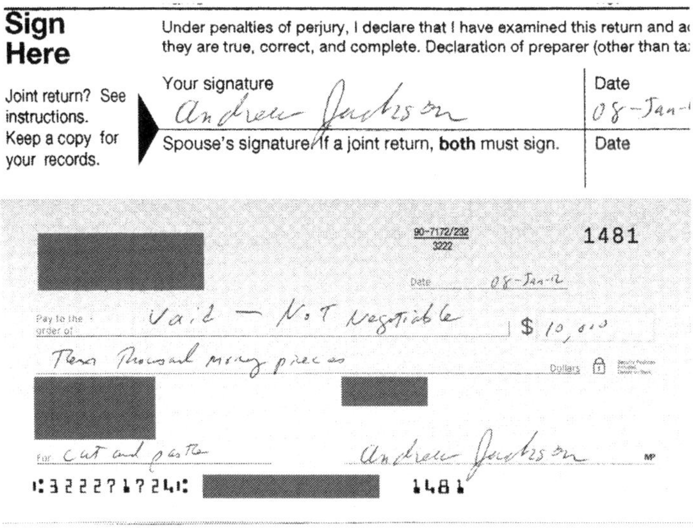

Figure 14 - Cut and Paste

Figure 15 - Cut and Paste Evidence

In Figure 14, the signature and date from the tax form were copied and pasted onto the signature line of the check. This was done using Adobe Photoshop™. The question is which is real, or are both signatures cut-and-paste from a third document. Unless an original document is examined, the document examiner may not be able to determine whether one is an original.

Cut and paste is determined by extracting both signatures then placing one on top of the other. If there is an exact match, one is a copy of the other or both are a copy of a third signature. In Figure 15, the signature of Andrew Jackson from the tax form is placed over the signature on the check. The example shows a slight offset in order to differentiate the two signatures which fit exactly over each other.

Altered Documents

White light

Infrared 850 nanometers light

Figure 16 - Infrared Light

A question may arise whether a document has been altered. An example is if a contract states a person owes $100. The person owed the money may add a line at the top of the 1 to make the contract appear to state person owes $700. In Figure 16, both portions of the seven were drawn in black ink. The eye may not be able to discern the alteration. A document examiner has several tools which allow differentiation of the inks. In this example, the seven was examined under infrared light at 850 nanometers frequency. The infrared clear-

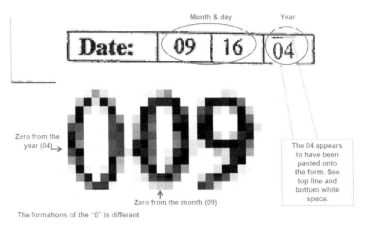

Month & day   Year

Zero from the year (04)

The 04 appears to have been pasted onto the form. See top line and bottom white space.

Zero from the month (09)

The formations of the "0" is different

Figure 17 - Altered Documents

ly shows two inks were used to construct the seven. The horizontal line virtually disappears under infrared light.

Document examiners also examine documents printed on computer printers or other mechanical devices. These documents may show signs of having been altered. In Figure 17, the year was changed. A person printed the number "04," cut out the "04" and then pasted it over the date on the document.

Several aspects show the document was altered. The line below the "04" shows a white section where the paper on which the "04" was printed covered the line. The "04" does not line up precisely with the baseline of the remainder of the date. Images on a computer are made of pixels. This stands for "picture element." The pixels are small dots. When we look at the image, the pixels blend to give the appearance of a solid image. When the characters were enlarged, the pixel formation of the number zero in the month differs from the pixel formation in the year. This shows they were printed using different printers or different fonts. This is another example where Photoshop™ is used to enlarge the image to reveal the pixel construction.

Toner Printer Example

Wax Printer Example

Figure 18 - Differences in Printers

A set of pages in a document may have been printed on different printers yet may be part of a true, correct document. As an example, perhaps text is printed on a laser printer, and the photographs are printed on a photographic printer. Document examiners must learn to differentiate different printing techniques.

It is possible that a person does not like the terms of a contract on a specific page. The person may type that page on a computer and print the new page with changed terms on a different printer using the same font as the original contract. The document examiner must be able to determine whether the added page is from a different printer. In Figure 18, the word "life-c" is printed on two types of common office printers. The same file was printed for each example. The fonts are identical for the toner and wax printer examples. The pages appear identical when they are viewed with the naked eye. The example is magnified 40 times with a digital microscope.

Robosigning

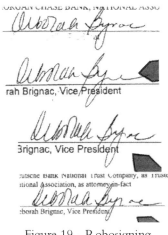

Figure 19 - Robosigning

Robosigning is where one person's name is on perhaps hundreds or thousands of documents yet the documents were signed by many different people who simulated the name. We do not know whether any of the documents were signed by the person whose signature appears in the signature line. Often these incidents occurred with mortgage loan documents.

In this case, the client presented to me 11 documents allegedly signed by the same person. Many of the signatures were very different from each other. The client wanted to know whether more than one person had executed the signatures, which were all the same name. The client had gone to the county recorder's office to obtain certified copies of deeds.

After reviewing each of the signatures, it was apparent that many were executed by different people. The signatures were followed by "/s" or initials indicating that another person had signed the name. After those signatures were removed from the set, four documents shown in Figure 19 remained with only a signature. Examination of these four signatures indicated they

47

Line by Line

were all signed by the same person. Since known signatures by the person whose name was on the signature line were not available, there was no way to know whether these four signatures were true signatures of the person.

Figure 20 - Rubber Stamp

Other examples of robosigning are performed with a rubber stamp. Figure 20 shows where the person signs the document by affixing a stamp that has a signature as part of the stamp. A pen is not used to sign the document.

Determine Line Sequence

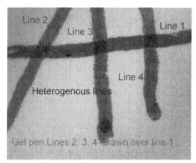

Figure 21 - Line Sequence Illusion

Determining line sequence means researching the question, "Which line came first?" Another question is whether someone added a signature over a line, or was the signature already on the page before markings were added.

Line sequence is determining which line came first

where two lines cross. This is a difficult problem for document examiners to solve. In cases where the same pen is used, indicators provide the document examiner means to determine the stroke sequence. Where different pens are used, it is often more difficult. Figure 21 shows black ink appears on top of blue ink, even where the blue ink is on top.

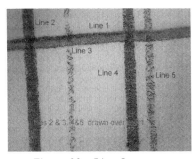

Figure 22 - Line Sequence

In the example in figure 22, using black gel pens, lines 2, 3 and 4 are drawn over line 1. We can't tell by just looking at the image. One indicator is a narrowing of a line where the top line crosses the bottom line. The appearance is similar to an hour glass shape. When the pen crosses the line, it dips into the groove formed by the first pen. This causes the narrowing. We need to use a microscope to find this. Sometimes the microscope will not reveal this either.

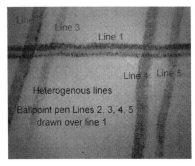

Figure 23 - Line Sequence Infrared

Alternate light methods can be used to differentiate the inks where two or more same color pens were used to alter a document. Figure 23 is an example of lines crossing viewed in infrared light. Note the horizontal line

49

appears on top even though it is on bottom.

Figure 24 - Infrared Luminescence

Figure 24 shows where two lines may appear to have been made with the same pen when viewed by the naked eye. Using infrared light may reveal distinct inks. In Figure 24, two black inks were photographed using infrared luminescence. The inks glow differently under the infrared luminescence. Our eyes see only a small portion of the electromagnetic spectrum. We see between 400 and 700 nanometers. These techniques allow the document examiner to see beyond that which our eye can see. If different inks are used, alternate lighting will often show the difference.

Sophisticated equipment, such as the VSC, may be needed to reveal these differences in ink and line sequence. There are times when even more sophisticated equipment that measures the thickness of the lines in nanometers is needed. This equipment is owned by university and government laboratories due to cost. When these tests are required, the document examiner may need to engage the services of a specialty laboratory to perform the examination.

Use of Adobe Photoshop™

Figure 25 - Signature Match

Photoshop™ is used to compare signatures and other writing between a questioned document and known documents. In Figure 25, the known signature is black and the questioned signature is red. The known signature was placed over the questioned signature to determine how well they comport with each other. We can see angles and stroke structure are similar.

Figure 26 - Photoshop for Exhibit

Photoshop™ is a valuable tool for creating demonstrative exhibits for court. Figure 26 shows the difference between questioned documents in a case. The writing is shown with annotations describing the exhibit. This exhibit shows how the different structures in the writing are similar across the questioned and known writings. Lines and annotations were added.

Photoshop™ was used in Figure 27 to reconstruct a document that was allegedly a photocopy of a document that had been torn. The right side of the tear was selected then moved to align with the left side. When the sections were aligned the printed portions

51

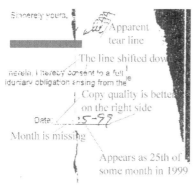

Figure 27 - Reconstruct a Ripped Document

Figure 28 - Hindi Writing

aligned, yet the written sections showed there was writing on the right section but no writing on the left section.

Document examiners can work with writing other than in their native language. I met a document examiner from India in China at the World Congress of Forensics. She asked me to assist with a case written in Hindi shown in Figure 28. Although I cannot read Hindi, I was able to discern anomalies between the known writing (identified with the letter A) and the questioned writing (identified with the letter D). In this case, Photoshop was used to place the known and questioned signatures onto the same page for ease of comparison and exhibition.

page for ease of comparison and exhibition.

Ink and Paper Dating

The analysis of ink can move beyond the skill set of the document examiner. An ink chemist may need to perform a chemical or spectral analysis of the ink to determine the composition of the ink. When the chemical composition is determined, it can be compared to ink libraries to identify the manufacturer and time range of manufacture of the ink. This technique is valuable to learn whether an ink existed at the time a document was signed. As an example, if a document is dated 1998 yet the ink was not manufactured until 2005, the document has been back-dated.

There may be times when a document examiner must consult a paper specialist to determine the age of paper on which a document is written or printed. Paper manufacturers insert watermarks into some paper. The watermarks are useful identifying the manufacturer and the approximate date range the paper was manufactured.

Photocopiers

Figure 29 - Trash Marks

Often photocopiers leave small dots called trash marks shown in figure 29. These may be visible only with a microscope rather than with the naked eye. Trash marks are caused by toner deposits. Document examiners look at this to determine whether the trash marks are in the same place on the pages. If they are in the same location, the same copier was probably used to create the document. If all pages of a document contain the same trash marks yet one page does not have the trash marks, the page was probably created on a different copier or printer than the other pages. Alternatively, they may have been created on the same copier or printer at different times. Some trash marks are the result of a speck of dust on the palatine. Others may be caused by a defect in the printing drum.

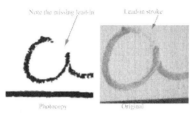

Figure 30 - Photocopy Problems

Photocopy machines may give false impressions about the document. An example shown in Figure 30 depicts when a portion of an image is written lightly using blue ink. Photocopy machines may not reproduce the lighter writing. The result is a false perception the writer wrote a letter with an open area or the lead-in stroke may be misinterpreted. In this example, I was first given a photocopy of the questioned document for examination. An anomaly seemed to be the writer of the questioned document wrote the letter "a" with an open top (left side image). When the original questioned document was examined, the light lead-in stroke was visible (right side image).

A question may arise whether pages of a document were created on the same photocopy machine. There are attributes of a photocopy machine that allow for determining whether a specific photocopy machine was used to copy an entire document or whether parts of the document were copied on different photocopy machines. Alternatively, the same photocopy machine may have been used at a later date after having been cleaned or worn parts replaced.

As an example the pages of a contract may have been reproduced on a photocopy machine. A question may arise whether someone did not like one of the terms of the contract, retyped the page and made a copy of the page to insert into the copy of the contract. Maybe the person made the copy of the page on a different photocopy machine. The photocopy machine has a photoreceptor drum. The drum is a metal belt covered by a semiconductor layer. If the drum has a defect, every time the drum turns to produce a page at the same location on a drum, the defect will show on the copied page. The film around the metal may pick up dust, chips, marks, toner and other debris. There may be dirt on the glass plate on which the document to be copied is placed. This dirt will show on each copy, and you can tell the copies were done at the same time.

A microscope may be needed to determine whether a signature on a document is ink or a photocopy of an ink signature. This question may arise when a black ink is used for the signature that looks the same as the black toner used to create the document on which the signature was made. The closeness of the black may deceive the eye. The top image on Figure 31 is a

Approximately 420x Magnification for Comparison

photocopy of the signature. The dot inside the line is not visible because it is created with photocopy toner. The bottom image demonstrates when another image is magnified, the dot inside the line is visible below the ink.

Figure 31 - Ink versus Toner

The Future of Document Examination

The future of document examination is a merger with computer forensics. So much is done on computers these days. Document examiners must learn aspects of analysis of digital images and signatures written on a digital signature pad. Sometimes document examiners are given documents that were scanned into a computer rather than the original paper documents.

Document examiners must examine computer-generated documents. Examples are scanned images and signatures made on digital signature pads, such as the ones used in retail stores. Digital signature pads are also used to sign legal documents, such as insurance forms, real estate forms, notarized forms etc. In these cases, an ink signature against which to compare the signature is not available. Instead, we have data that was captured by the digital tablet This starts to merge forensic document examination with computer fo-rensics.

Figure 32 - Signtature on a Digital Tablet

Figure 32 is an example of a writing written on a digi-tal tablet with no visual feedback for the writing other than watching the computer screen. The writing ap-pears somewhat rough because the image is captured by the tablet requesting data points at regular intervals. This is called "polling." Different tablets poll at differ-ent rates. The writing is stored as data points that can be plotted to display the writing or signature. Figure 33 is an example showing the beginning data points from the writing in Figure 33. The document examiner can calculate the time required to execute the writing. Figure 32 took 5.33 sec-onds to write.

388	361
388	360
388	360
388	360
388	359
388	358
387	356
386	355
383	355
378	355
372	356

Figure 33 - Data Points

The data points in figure 33 can be displayed as a plot as shown in figure 34. The plot can display markers at the location of the data points as shown in figure 35. Since the tab-let polls the data points at a constant rate, the data points show where the writer writes fast and slowly. Figure 34 allows the document examiner to learn the sequence in which the writing was executed. The long lines between data marks are locations where the writer lifted the pen. The dot between the first two long lines is the dot for the "i" in "signature."

The value of performing these analyses is the document examiner can obtain samples of writing from a person who claims not to have written a signature or a person suspected of having written a signature. The plots of the writing can be compared to learn whether the writing patterns are the same of very similar. This scientific approach removes much of the subjectivity from analyzing signatures.

Therefore, when a person signs a digital tablet, the document examiner has more evidence on which to base an opinion of authorship than when an ink on paper writing is executed.

Figure 33 shows the plot of the data points captured by the digital pen and tablet when the writer wrote the text in Figure 32. Figure 35 shows an expanded

Figure 34 - Plot of Electronically Captured Writing

view of the first part of the writing in figure 34. In Figure 34, the location of the data points is visible. The document examiner can determine the exact stroke sequence and writing direction used to execute the writing. Places where the writer lifted the pen are seen. Since the time between data points is constant, the document examiner can see where the writer moved rapidly and slowly. Nothing is left for inference.

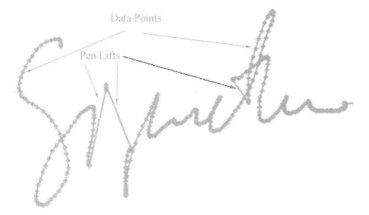

Figure 35 - Plot of Writing Showing Data Points

Chapter 5 – Develop a Standard Operating Procedure

Each document examiner develops a laboratory procedure best suited for the document examiner. When audits are performed in regulated industries, the auditor examines whether the company is following the stated procedures and whether the procedure follows the stated standards that are the basis of the procedure. The standards become the basis of the individual laboratory procedures.

A document examiner can develop a standard operating procedure (SOP) for his/her laboratory. The SOP can be based on a common standard such as ASTM standards. So long as the document examiner follows the stated SOP, which is based on a common standard, the document examiner is using a generally accepted practice that does not bias the results of the examination. The SOP may describe what the document examiner does when contacted for a new case, how the documents are handled when received, how they are stored and protected etc. The SOP also describes the standard procedure used to examine documents. It may describe what the examiner looks for during an examination.

The first thing I do is catalog the documents and provide unique identifier numbers to each. The next task is scanning the documents into the computer using a flatbed scanner at either 600 or more pixels per inch (PPI). The documents are stored in a tagged information file format (TIFF), which has no loss of resolution due to compression. Some document examiners use JPG file format. JPG compresses the file resulting in loss of resolution. The TIFF is a huge file. Color 8.5" x 11" scanned pages at 600 PPI are sometimes more than 100 megabytes in size.

Each document is examined for clarity. If the document has not scanned at a quality that is usable, the document is noted as not usable. If the questioned document(s) are not usable, the analysis cannot be performed.

After the files are scanned into the computer, I extract the writing that is to be examined from the pages using Photoshop™. Often this is a signature. The known writing is collected onto a single sheet in order to examine the writing for common traits and differences. The questioned writing is then extracted from the questioned documents and placed onto the page with the known writing. The questioned writing will often be changed to a color different from the color of the known writing. This makes identification of the questioned writing simple. A copy of the questioned writing is made to use for comparison with the known writing.

The questioned writing is set to a size that matches

the known writing. The questioned writing is placed on top of the known writing to compare the two for similarities and differences.

When common features are discovered in the known writing, the image of those features is enlarged to learn the details of the way the writing strokes were formed. Features, such as connections between letters, initial and terminal strokes, are examined. Relative sizes are often measured to determine whether there is consistency in the intra-writer variability.

Essentially, the examination starts at a gross level then works to a more detailed analysis. The gross-level examination is used to determine whether a more detailed analysis is necessary.

The document examiner's SOP includes asking questions of the client to determine the source of the questioned document and exemplars. As an example, the document examiner may need to learn whether the suspected writer of the questioned document had access to the writing instrument used to execute the document. This may be a type of pen, typewriter, printer etc. The document examiner may ask the client whether other potential authors of the questioned document may have had access to the instrument used to create the questioned writing or document.

Chapter 6 – Are Document Examiners Better Than Laypeople at Identifying Handwriting?

Michael Risinger, law professor at Seton Hall University and Michael Saks, professor of law at Arizona State University, assert the ability of forensic document examiners may be no better than laypersons at identifying the author of questioned writing. They claim document examination fails the test of application of the scientific method. They critiqued the studies performed demonstrating superior ability of trained document examiners to identify or eliminate the author of a questioned writing.

Discussion

Risinger and Saks (1996) discussed the acceptance of expert witnesses in the courts. The 1923 Frye decision stated the methods presented by the expert are judged by the general acceptance of the methods within the scientific community. The later 1993 Daubert decision requires the expert's presentation must meet specific scientific criteria of falsifiability, or refutability or testability. The Starzecpyzel (1995) decision excluded document examiners from the Daubert criteria by classifying document examiners as "skilled experts" rather than scientists. The Starzecpyzel Court stated, "In sum, the Court is convinced that forensic document examiners may be of assistance to you. However, their skill is practical in nature, and despite anything you may hear or have heard, it does not have the demonstrable certainty that some sciences have." Mary Wenderoth Kelly, the document examiner in Starzecpyzel case, was unable to provide quantifiable methods by which to demonstrate differences between writers. The Starzecpyzel Court wrote:

"If forensic document examination does rely on an underlying principle, logic dictates the principle must embody the notion that inter-writer differences, even when intentionally suppressed, can be distinguished from natural variation. How FDEs might accomplish this was unclear to the Court before the hearing, and largely remains so after the hearing."

The document examination community began to develop research to demonstrate that document examination, specifically handwriting examination, is a science-based discipline.

Risinger's and Saks' assert the Starzecpyzel Court was correct in its statement that document examination is not based on science. Risinger and Saks contend that document examination is not a repeatable and verifiable discipline. Risinger and Saks attempted to discredit Kam et al.'s (1994) research testing document examiners' ability at identifying and excluding the author of a questioned document by using scientifically sound methods.

The basis of handwriting identification is no two people write exactly alike and the natural variation within an individual's writing is consistent. Risinger and Saks state that handwriting examination is, "not based on standardized measurements of any precision." This individuality has been demonstrated by such authors as Osborne (1929), Hilton (1993, 1995) and Harrison (1981).

Osborne (1929) in chapter VII, "Special Instruments, Measures and Appliances" described several standard measurements. Osborne recognized the need to, "Investigate the question of identity in size, proportions and position in various parts of a model signature and of one or more traced imitations" (p. 83). Osborne states, "The principle underlying the identification of a handwriting is the same as that by which anything with a great number of possible variations is identified as belonging to a certain class or a particular thing" (p. 225). Osborne (1929) concedes writing can be that of another yet when all of the identifying attributes are considered, we can expect that, "it is practically impossible" (p. 226). Hilton (1993) reiterates Osborne's point stating that identification of a writer is established by identification of sufficient identifying factors as, "… their having originated at two different sources is so unlikely that for practical purposes it can be considered nonexistent" (p. 9). Hilton (1995) stated mathematics is a tool in the scientific approach. Harrison (1981) wrote, "Where a wide range of identifying characteristics exists, identification can be largely objective, so that opinions as to authorship of handwriting cannot be dismissed as guesses … on the part of the document examiner" (p. 292).

Risinger and Saks stated the concept of individuality of each person's writing is "nonscience metaphysical statements" (p. 9). Mary Wenderoth Kelly, the document examiner, in the Starzecpyzel case was unable to provide a standard by which either intra-writer variability or inter-writer variability can be expressed. Risinger and Saks interpret this inability to quantify the variability as metaphysical, or outside the realm of science. This book has shown intra-writer variability is measurable.

Basing their analysis on the findings of Ms. Kelly, Risinger and Saks state that handwriting identification, "… is not based on standardized measurements of any precision." Osborne (1929) demonstrated the use of precise measures of writing size, slant, spacing and other characteristics to assist with identification. Harrison (1981) described the need to measure the characteristics of writing in order to distinguish the intra-writer variability. Srihari et al. (2002) developed validated measurement techniques for the purpose of demonstrating individuality of handwriting. Srihari et al. were able to validate individuality at a 95 percent confidence level. Huber and Hedrick (1999) developed 21 measurable characteristics of writing that together identify the writer. These findings contradict Risinger's and Saks' (1996) contention that writing cannot be individually distinguished by using quantifiable and repeatable methods.

Challenges to Validity of Document Examination

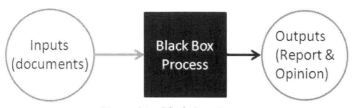

Figure 36 – Black Box Process

Risinger's and Saks' statement that validation of hand-writing identification techniques is not scientific and requires "black box" (p. 10) validation is refutable. The concept of a "black box" (shown in Figure 36) implies that inputs and outputs are known while the processing method is unknown. In the case of the document examiner, this implies the documents to be examined and the report are known, while the method of examination is unknown. This concept ignores the existence of the wealth of literature and standards, such as the ASTM standards that describe methods for examination of documents. Risinger and Saks asked, "What evidence, if any, exists to show that document examiners can accurately identify or exclude authorship by comparison of hands, or do so better than the average person?" (p. 10) They answered the rhetorical question with, "almost none" (p. 10).

Risinger and Saks (1996) reference a study by Kam et al. (1994). Kam et al. sought to test the results of a literature search by Risinger et al. in 1989. Risinger et al (1989) questioned the validity of handwriting examination as a tool for law enforcement and compared handwriting examination expertise to folk medicine and astrology. Rather than attempting to refute the results of the Kam et al. study based on the experimental design, Risinger and Saks (1996) developed a hypothesis. The motivation of the two experimental groups in Kam et al.'s study differ. Kam et al.'s test group consisted of 7 FBI laboratory document examiners. The control group consisted of 10 graduate students from Drexel University. Risinger and Saks argue the control group was less motivated to perform well on the test, thus giving less successful results. Risinger and Saks failed to show evidence of motivation of the subjects affecting the results of the experiment. Kam et al. concluded that, "… professional document examiners from the Federal Bureau of Investigation are significantly better in performing writer identification than college-educated nonexperts" (p. 13). Risinger and Saks conceded, "The performance of the FBI document examiners was remarkable" (p. 21).

Laboratory error in five tests conducted by the Forensic Sciences Foundation in 1984-1987 is cited by Risinger and Saks (1989, 1996 p. 10-13). The inherent error of the laboratories does not support the theory that there is no scientific basis for handwriting identification. Risinger and Saks fail to explore the testing methods that were used by the laboratories. Without this information, drawing a valid conclusion as to the results is not possible. A comparison must be made of the methods that yielded a correct result and those that resulted in an erroneous result. Perhaps the more scientific methods would have yielded the correct results and the more subjective methods yielded the incorrect results. By failing to explore test methods, Risinger and Saks support their contention that document examination is a "black box."

In 2009 the National Academy of Sciences issued a report that called for a more scientific approach to forensic sciences (National Research Council, 2009). Forensic document examination was included in the report. The essence of the report is that use of subjective methods and laboratory bias has yielded incorrect results in the various forensic disciplines. This statement supports Saks' and Risinger's observation that a scientific method must be applied to document examination. Conversely, it does not support the hypothesis that scientific methods are not used by document examiners. Subjective analysis by document examiners can yield incorrect results as shown by the difficulty document examiners had differentiating simulated and disguised writing (Found and Rogers, 2008). Found and Rogers stated, "… the misleading rate for the disguise category of questioned signatures is very high due to the strategy of observing dissimilar features and concluding this equates to a different writer" (p. 58). The results of Found and Rogers do not purport that a scientific method is not used by document examiners. It shows the need for refinement of the methods applied in a specific type of examination. Found and Rogers (2008) reported the study that was performed with qualified document examiners resulted in "… a correct called (CC) percentage of 92.2% and a misleading called (MC) percentage of 7.8%" (p. 56).

Dyer et al. (2006) conducted a study to examine the strategy that is used by trained document examiners and laypeople when examining signatures. The control group (lay people) was trained for 30 minutes on signature analysis. Dyer et al. reported, "that FDE subjects perform significantly better on signature tasks than do lay people" (p. 1402). The document examiners were shown to apply better cognitive skills and focus on the significance and weight of features rather than focusing on single features as did the lay subjects. Dyer et al. demonstrated a repeatable and quantifiable approach used by document examiners.

In Crisp (2003), the Fourth Circuit Court of Appeals ruled, "The fact that handwriting comparison analysis has achieved widespread and lasting acceptance in the expert community gives us the assurance of reliability that *Daubert* requires" (p. 10). Denbeaux and Risinger (2003) ignored this ruling in their presentation of a brief history of the admissibility of handwriting expertise in the courts. In reference to appellate decisions on handwriting evidence, Denbeaux and Risinger wrote, "The appellate decisions all managed to find no abuse of discretion without describing the particular claim of expertise which was at stake in the case" (p. 36).

Conclusion

Although Risinger and Saks cite the study by Kam et al., which concluded document examiners showed statistically significant better results than laypeople at identification of writers, the results of the Kam et al. (1994) are ignored. Risinger and Saks conceded, "The performance of the FBI document examiners [in the Kam et al. study] was remarkable" (p. 21).

Several researchers have demonstrated scientifically based methods that have been successful in correctly solving document examination problems. Researchers, such as Srihari et al., Hilton (1995) and Kam et al., Dyer et al. and Found and Rogers, have demonstrated that application of scientific methods to document examination yields successful results.

Chapter 7 – Document Examiners Must Meet Legal Standards

Federal Rules of Evidence Rule 702

In the United States, there are 2 basic legal standards for expert witnesses to meet in order to qualify to testify in court: 1) In federal court under Federal Rules of Evidence 702 is used, and 2) States have state codes for determining whether an expert is qualified to testify.

FRE Rule 702 states:

"A witness who is qualified as an expert by knowledge, skill, experience, training, or education may testify in the form of an opinion or otherwise if:

(a) the expert's scientific, technical, or other specialized knowledge will help the trier of fact to understand the evidence or to determine a fact in issue;

(b) the testimony is based on sufficient facts or data;

(c) the testimony is the product of reliable principles and methods; and

(d) the expert has reliably applied the principles and methods to the facts of the case."

These requirements are restated in ASTM Standard E444, Scope of Work of Forensic Document Examiners. ASTM standard E2388, Minimum Training Requirements for Forensic Document Examiners provides a syllabus for the training and education needed by forensic document examiners.

Frye v. United States

In the 1923 case, Frye v. United States, 54 App. D.C. 46, 47, 293 F. 1013, 1014 (1923), the United States Supreme Court stated that expert opinion based on a scientific technique is inadmissible unless the technique is "generally accepted" as reliable in the relevant scientific community. Many states, including California, apply the Frye standard.

In the November 26, 2012 ruling in Sargon Enterprises, Inc. v. University of Southern California, the California Supreme Court cited Daubert and FRE 702 in excluding the testimony of a business valuation expert as being speculative in estimating potentially lost profits. Writing the unanimous opinion, California Supreme Court Justice Ming Chin wrote, "The trial court properly acted as a gatekeeper to exclude speculative expert testimony. Its ruling came within its discretion." Without adopting the Federal Rule 702 or Daubert standard, the California Supreme Court took a step in the direction of the judge as gatekeeper and moving away from Frye. Judge Chin cited Rule 702 in his opinion.

Daubert v. Merrill–Dow Pharmaceuticals

In 1993, a case decided by the United States Supreme Court defined the requirements for expert testimony.

- Has the scientific theory been tested?

- Has the scientific theory been peer reviewed and published?

- What is the potential error rate?

- Do standards and controls exist and are they maintained?

- Has the theory and body of knowledge been generally accepted in the relevant industry?

The Daubert ruling was applied to Rule 702.

Testing requires establishing a hypothesis. Empirical

tests are conducted to determine the validity of the hypothesis. The Daubert court cited authorities stating, "'The criterion of the scientific status of a theory is its falsifiability, or refutability, or testability.'" Testing the refutability of a hypothesis means we try to disprove the hypothesis rather than prove the hypothesis. Attempting to demonstrate the hypothesis is correct may result in a confirmation bias. Confirmation bias means the researcher focuses on information confirming the hypothesis and rejects information conflicting with the hypothesis.

The expert must show the methodology used to arrive at an opinion can be tested and repeated by others. The theories applied to the research methodology should have been published in peer reviewed journals demonstrating other people in the field have said this is an acceptable methodology.

The question of error rate in the field is difficult for document examiners to determine. Document examiners can take proficiency tests to determine performance on a controlled test. Performance on one or even a few tests does not set the standard for error rates. If a person correctly answers 95 percent of the answers on a test, this is the error rate for the test. It is not necessarily reflective of overall performance. The same is true if a person scores 80 percent on a test. The person may solve all answers correctly on another test.

Studies have been conducted at universities to ascertain error rates of document examiners versus lay people when examining signatures. A question whether controlled studies are equivalent to field performance has not been answered. Huber and Hedrick (1999) address the question of error rate by examining the likelihood ratio. A difficulty with this approach is determining the frequency of occurrence in an overall population.

In Daubert, the judge is the gatekeeper. States, such as California, apply the Frye standard for admissibility of experts. These states recognize the judge cannot have sufficient knowledge of every discipline to determine whether the expert is truly knowledgeable of the subject matter to act as a gatekeeper. Frye requires the expert to apply generally accepted practices.

U.S. versus Starzecpyzel stated document examination is not a science because of the difficulty determining error rates. The result was document examination was ruled as not a science. It does not have published error rates and is not published in journals of pure science. The result is document examination was not subject to Daubert.

Kumho Tire v. Carmichael 526 U.S. 137 (1999) ruled expert testimony must follow proper technique. The court ruled Daubert applies to all expert testimony, not just scientific testimony. The judge is given flexibility in allowing acceptance of expert testimony. Therefore, forensic document examiners are subject to the Daubert standards when testifying as an expert witness in federal court.

Chapter 8 – Importance of Following Generally Accepted Practices

There are several abilities to look for when selecting a forensic document examiner as an expert witness or consultant that can help improve the chances of prevailing with your case, provided your client's claim is meritorious. One of your key requirements should be the document examiner follows a generally accepted practice for forensic document examiners.

In Frye v. U.S., 293 F.2d 1013 (D.C. CA 1923), the D.C. Court of Appeals adopted the test for "general acceptance." As relevant in California, the Kelly rule, People v. Kelly (1976) 17 Cal.3d 24, provides expert testimony must be based on a technique that is "sufficiently established to have gained general acceptance in the particular field to which it belongs."

I testified in a case where the opposing side's expert witness document examiner failed to follow generally accepted practice for handwriting identification of a questioned signature. As a result, the court ruled in a bench trial the petitioner's document expert was more credible than the respondent's expert. The attorney who hired me prevailed in the case.

As with any other profession, document examiners have a range of expertise and experience. As important as it is for your client to make a clear assessment of your abilities, it is up to you to determine in advance and with a high degree of accuracy whether the document examiner you plan to hire will perform the most accurate assessments and be ready to back up those assessments with a scientifically repeatable sound methodology in court.

An individual can only be eliminated as the writer of a questioned document when the range of variability of the known writer has been determined. Established authorities state that a sufficient number of samples are required to show this variability. In this particular case, the other document examiner eliminated the decedent as the writer of a holographic will based on observed differences between two known signatures and the questioned signature. Two samples are not sufficient to demonstrate a writer's range of variability. The examiner failed to state there were also differences between the two known signatures, which were stipulated to have been written contemporaneously (in this case during the same sitting) by the decedent.

In accepted methodology, the basis of writer identification is determination of both similar and dissimilar traits in the questioned writing and the known writings. Additionally, the variability in the handwriting of the author of the known writings must be analyzed.

Based on these findings, only then can it be determined with a degree of accuracy the extent to which the questioned writing has the same traits as and falls within the known variability of the known writing.

The opposing examiner in this case made no effort to determine the variability of the decedent's known handwriting. She made no attempt to examine the original will that was available in the court's records room. I examined the original holographic will as required by the ASTM standard E2290 and displayed the scanned copy as an exhibit.

The other examiner failed to point out attributes of the questioned writing which also existed in the known writing. This provided a strong probability the will had been written by the decedent.

My exhibits were presented with 18 examples of the decedent's known handwriting. Many of these displayed attributes the other document examiner erroneously stated were not found in the questioned writing.

In this case, the other examiner failed to follow either standard ASTM E2290-07, *Standard Guide for Examination of Handwritten Items*, or any other generally accepted methodology. In this standard, item 7.5 states, "Determine whether the questioned writing is original writing. If it is not original writing, request the original." The standard states if the reproduction is not of "sufficient clarity for comparison purposes, discontinue these procedures." The examiner used a scanned image of a photo reduction of the original document. The original document showed characteristics that were not visible in this reproduction. Had the oppos-ing examiner followed generally accepted practice by examining all of the known writing I examined, it is possible the other examiner may have reached a dif-ferent opinion than the opinion she stated.

It is important for an attorney to ask an expert to describe the methodology to be used researching the case. Ensure the methodology is generally accepted in the industry. The prospective document examin-er should be able to cite authorities that support the claim the methodology is accepted in the practice of forensic document examination.

Chapter 9 – Can Forensic Experts Overcome Their Biases?

Research shows document examiners who work for the government tend to focus on differences in writing, whereas private practice document examiners tend to focus on similarities in writing (McAlexander 1999).

There is a Zen saying, "When the flower arranger arranges the flowers, he also arranges his mind and the mind of the person who looks at the flowers." As document examiners, we arrive at an opinion whether a document is authentic or not authentic. Bias can come into play. The bias starts when document examiners are hired by an attorney. The attorney approaches the document examiner saying, "I have a case where I need to show my client wrote this check so he is due the money," or "my client did not sign this contract so he has no obligation under it." This sets the bias. One of the jobs of a document examiner is to take a step back and disengage from the bias. This can be done by taking a step back from the scope of the examination request and focusing on the evidence. Application of a qualitative scientific approach reduces cognitive bias.

The document examiner cares about the writing on the document, potential alterations or other attributes of the analysis. A document examiner may review the document for typographical or grammatical errors to determine the potential educational or literacy level of the writer. The document examiner may not be interested in the contents of the court case. The only point of interest is the documents. Specifics of the origin or history of the documents may be requested by the document examiner. Too much knowledge may induce cognitive or unconscious bias. As soon as I arrange my mind, I am arranging the attorney's mind.

None of us wants to feel our opinions are tainted by bias. The ability to recognize when bias is an influence in an expert's opinion and the skill of an expert to overcome his or her biases is integral to an expert's credibility.

Experts make decisions that are expressed as opinions by applying analytical methods developed through training, education and practice. Such prior experience may induce biases that cause the expert to use trusted methods without considering alternatives. Forensic science seeks to produce reliable evidence which is clearly reported (Sjerps & Meester 2009). Experts must recognize when their biases and those of others influence their decisions.

Black's Law Dictionary defines bias as, "Inclination; prejudice; predilection (Garner, 2009)." Prior experiences, learning paradigms, individual beliefs, and other biases can cloud the understanding of what is important. There are two types of bias: cognitive bias and motivational bias (Giannelli, 2008). Cognitive biases, which occur at the subconscious level, frequently interfere with the ability of people to make good decisions. Motivational bias, which can occur at the conscious or subconscious level, results from a person's desire to deliver expected results.

Experts work in private, crime or other forms of laboratories. ASTM reported that 80 percent of studied laboratories showed laboratory bias (Lawrey, 2009). Twenty percent of the laboratories displayed "significantly high bias." This bias was the result of interactions among many people. Griffen and Tversky (1992) attributed similar bias to people's tendency toward being more overconfident in their judgments than is warranted by the facts. When we select evidence that is not independent of the forensic analysis, problems occur (Sjerps & Meester, 2009). Schwab (2008) showed that bias induces experts to be overconfident in rating their abilities.

The National Academy of Sciences (NAS) (National Research Council, 2009) reported that bias is a severe problem in forensic sciences. Cognitive biases were described as, "common features of decision making, and they cannot be willed away." NAS reported that judges are subject to bias in their rulings. The NAS report cites studies that half the fingerprint examinations had bias introduced into the procedures. A recommendation is made to remove the association of crime laboratories from police agencies to reduce the motivational bias (National Research Council 2009).

The expert bias can be reduced if the expert is not aware of the side which has hired him or her (Baer, 2005).

Research demonstrates that awareness of the source of cognitive bias is insufficient to prevent a person from being trapped by biases (Ariely 2008, Cialdini 2001). Arzy, Brezis, Khoury, Simon and Ben-Hur (2009) discovered that by including one misleading detail about a patient, cases were misdiagnosed in 90 percent of cases by practicing physicians. Telling a control group there was one misleading detail did not reduce the diagnostic error. When the misleading detail was omitted from the information, the misdiagnosis reduced to 30 percent (Arzy et al., 2009). Document examiners must sort through evidence so as not to follow the trail of misleading information which results in a flawed opinion.

The presentation of the information is known as framing. When a problem is framed in a manner that appears to be logically sound, the problem solver will accept the framing and attempt to solve the problem in conjunction with the way the problem is framed (Bernstein, 1996). A study was conducted at Stanford University to test the impact of framing a situation then adding additional information about the decision that is to be made. Subjects were given sufficient information regarding a courtroom trial (Kahneman and Tversky, 1995). One group was given more detail regarding the defendant, and another group was given additional information regarding the plaintiff. Although the groups knew the data was biased, they were unable to mentally balance the information. The biased groups were more confident about the outcome in favor of the side whose information was more voluminous than the group with balanced information (Kahneman and Tversky, 1995).

Webber (2008) reported, "Juries ... typically base their decisions on whichever story seems most plausible to them, rather than weighing the evidence." These decisions are made regardless of whether the information is accurate. McAuliff, Kovera and Nunez (2009) expanded on Webber's findings, stating that when jurors' motivation is low or their ability to understand the presented information is poor, they rely on heuristics and that which they understand as real-life situations (McAuliff et al., 2009). McAuliff et al. discovered that jurors are, "Insensitive to the presence of a confound or experimenter bias in the expert's research," yet the jurors relied on their flawed analysis of the expert's evidence when rendering a verdict.

A sharp attorney can bias a jury by framing questions to the witness. Framing bias can cause the jury to view the expert as qualified or not qualified. McAuliff et al. (2009) found a positive relationship between verdicts and juror's evaluation of expert's evidence. McAuliff et al. reported that jurors are not able to evaluate statistical evidence and methodologies. They also reported that, "Judges are unable to differentiate between valid and junk science ..." leading to, admission of invalid research at trial." The document examiner must reduce these potential biases by presenting clear and easy to understand evidence to support an opinion.

Science does not prove something is true. Science shows evidence something is true. Rigorous science always attempts to find evidence contradicting accepted fact. Only when attempts to demonstrate contradictory evidence fail, does the scientist continue to accept the fact.

A difference between working a document examination case and a true scientific study is a scientific study is generally conducted double blind where neither the researcher nor the subject knows whether they are receiving real or counterfeit material. In document examination cases, the hiring attorney generally describes the purpose of the analysis, thus imposing a bias the document examiner needs to overcome. An attorney may tell the document examiner, "My client says he did not sign this document." The null hypothesis may state, "The writer of the questioned document is the writer of the known documents". The objective of the research is to refute this hypothesis by showing the writer of the known document did not write the questioned document. If the hypothesis cannot be refuted, it is accepted.

Chapter 10 – Document Examiner's Reports

The result of the document examiner's research is a report of the findings and opinion. Clients do not always want a report if the findings fail to support the necessary position of the case. The report is probably discoverable.

An alternative to a report is a letter of opinion. A letter of opinion is a brief statement outlining the method used and opinion reached from the examination. The letter of opinion lists the questioned document(s) and known documents examined. The letter of opinion may also be discoverable.

A report must demonstrate the document examiner applied a scientific approach using generally accepted practices to the analysis.

A report must state the opinion as an affidavit. Some jurisdictions require the report as an exhibit to the affidavit. Federal court has clear requirements stated in federal Rules of Civil Procedure Rule 26(a)(2)(B). Failure to follow the federal rules in federal court may result in denial of the report as evidence in federal court. State courts may have specific rules for expert reports.

Although these sections may not be mandatory in state court, it is helpful for the document examiner to use a format similar to the format here.

1. Cover page – State the scope of the report and the opinion. This allows the reader to understand the summary without paging through the report.

2. Detailed scope of the examination. An out of scope statement may help clarify the boundaries of the research examination. An example of an in-scope and out of scope statement may be, "We want you to examine the signature fro authenticity. We do not want you to examine the machine printed text." The signature is in scope. The machine printed text is out of scope.

3. Summary of the documents examined

   a. One section for questioned

   b. One section for known

   c. For each document include

      i. The identification code

      ii. Date of the document or "unknown"

      iii. Type of document

      iv. Original, copy, fax etc.

      v. Form of writing (print, cursive, manuscript, mixed)

4. Assumptions

5. Limitations

6. Methodology used in the examination

7. Results of the examination

    a. Similarities

    b. Differences

8. Conclusion / Opinion

9. Affidavit

10. Exhibits

    a. Document examiner's CV

    b. Questioned document(s)

    c. Known document(s)

    d. Supporting images showing how the opinion was reached

    e. Any other exhibits to support the methodology and conclusion

Chapter 11 - Selecting A Document Examiner

The Internet provides an invaluable source for finding a qualified document examiner for your case. Search engines such as Google, Yahoo, Bing etc. provide ease in finding document examiners. Location on the search page does not necessarily mean the person is qualified to perform the work. It is incumbent on the attorney or other prospective employer of the document examiner to ensure the document examiner has the required background and is free of potential liabilities which may arise in deposition or trial.

Once a prospective document examiner is found, use the Internet search engines to learn about the document examiner. Type the document examiner's name and company name into the search engine. The attorney on the other side of the case will probably perform this task. This is a good means to validate the information contained in the examiner's CV. Examine the organizations of which the document examiner is a member to determine whether they are legitimate.

Often the first question an attorney asks the document examiner is, "How much does it cost to examine a signature (or other subject of the examination)?"

This is the wrong question. An honest document examiner will not be able to answer this question without seeing the case. Most document examiners charge an hourly rate. The cost depends on the complexity of the case. Most document examiners charge a minimum nonrefundable retainer fee. This is similar to a prospective client asking an attorney to quote the complexity of a case before the attorney has seen the details of the case.

Ask the document examiner to forward a retainer agreement and fee schedule. A good fee schedule will have a simple calculation method rather than a complex structure of different fees for different work. Often, there is a rate for research and travel and a second rate for testimony.

Deliverables You Can Expect from the Document Examiner

- **Continuous communication:** The document examiner must communicate with the client about all aspects of the case. The document examiner becomes an integral part of the theme of your case. He or she must understand your theme and be able to communicate how the research integrates and supports your case theme. The other side is the client must communicate with the document examiner. This includes proper preparation prior to all testimony. Preparation must be done ahead of testimony rather than the day of testimony. Early preparation allows the attorney and witness time to resolve any potential difficulties and reflect on the preparation.

- **Timely attention to your case:** The document examiner must meet all required milestones for case deliverables. Make sure the document examiner is able to dedicate the required time to your case.

- **Instructions for obtaining necessary documents for research:** The document examiner will provide instructions for obtaining exemplars for the case. This ensures the case is sound and not subject to challenge due to improper exemplars.

- **A comprehensive report:** The report must be complete, describing all methods used, reasons for the opinion reached and list all supporting exhibits. The report must comply with all applicable rules of court for the jurisdiction.

- **Questions to ask the opposing examiner:** The document examiner will review the report from the opposing examiner and generate questions to ask the opposing examiner in deposition of cross examination.

- **Questions to ask the document examiner on direct examination:** The document examiner will prepare a list of questions to ask on direct examination. These questions include areas of potential weakness in the examiner's background or the examination methodology. Asking these questions on direct examination allows the examiner to answer the questions in a friendly environment rather than on cross examination.

Questions to ask a Prospective Document Examiner

1. Federal Rules of Evidence 702, California Evidence Code 720(a) and ASTM Standard E444 all state an expert must be able to demonstrate skill, special knowledge, education, experience or training in the field in which the expert testifies. **Ask the prospective document examiner how he or she qualifies according to these requirements.** Note the conjunction *or* between the requirements. Only one is required, yet more than one is better and all five is best.

2. **Describe your training and education in document examination and related subjects.** ASTM Standard E2388 outlines the minimum training and education requirements for forensic document examiners. The National Academy of Sciences stated training is secondary to education for the forensic sciences.

3. **Is the document examiner trained in research methods and science?** Document examiners are researchers. They need to apply a science-based approach to the case. Ask the pro-

spective document examiner to describe the scientific method.

4. **Describe your methodology.** Learn how the document examiner conducts research. Is the methodology based on a generally accepted practice in the industry? Is the methodology repeatable by another document examiner in a manner that another examiner can reach the same conclusion when the methodology is followed? Is there a standard operating procedure for the methodology?

5. **Can the document examiner demonstrate specialized knowledge of the discipline?** Can the document examiner cite authorities to support the opinion, or is the opinion simply based on the document examiner's belief? Does the document examiner know the source of the information that supports the opinion?

6. **Does the document examiner publish in peer reviewed journals or present at conferences before peers?**

7. **Does the document examiner perform research in the field of forensic document examination? Is the research presented to peers for review?**

8. **What is the document examiner's education that supports the ability to perform forensic document examination?** Education may be in

document examination and related subjects. Some related subjects are chemistry for performing ink analysis, physics to understand analysis using different light frequencies, physiology to understand the motor coordination of writing, computer imaging for analyzing digital images and many others. Education must always include comprehensive education in forensic document examination. Ask the document examiner how he or she remains current in the field.

9. **What format is used for your report?** A report needs to be clear and succinct. Long, voluminous reports are difficult to read and understand. The report needs to be written in language understandable to the layperson rather than the reader of a professional journal.

10. **What types of demonstrative exhibits are created?** Demonstrative exhibits show the trier of fact how the opinion was reached. Properly prepared exhibits can educate the trier of fact to the development and underlying basis of an expert's opinion.

11. **Is the document examiner certified?** Ask the document examiner whether he or she is certified by a document examination organization. Private examiners are certified by National Association of Document Examiners whereas examiners with government experience may be certified by the Board of Forensic Document Examiners. Other document examiners may hold a university level

certificate in forensic document examination. Any of these demonstrates a high level of specialized training. Be careful of people who hold a certification from a "diploma mill." There is an organization which supplies people who have two-year memberships, 15 hours of classes from the organization and $250 with a "diplomate" status. This organization does not list document examination on its web site, yet there are document examiners who have a diplomate certificate from this organization.

12. **Does the document examiner stay current in the discipline?** Conferences and university classes are excellent ways for the document examiner to maintain currency in the field. Most conferences offer full-day hands-on workshops in conjunction with the conference.

13. **Ask the document examiner for a copy of a current CV**

Chapter 12 – Conclusion

Forensic document examination is a technical discipline requiring the examiner to have a high degree of skill. Variability of writing cannot be determined by a simple visual examination. The experience, knowledge and skill of a trained document examiner is needed to identify and articulate the intricacies that define a common or not common author.

Tools and techniques used by skilled document examiners today are different and more precise than those used by document examiners in the past. Advances in computer hardware and software provide means of more precisely comparing handwriting than previously difficult and cumbersome methods. Powerful digital microscopes combined with software such as Adobe Photoshop permit document examiners to quickly learn the intricacies of a document, letter by letter. When hiring a document examiner as a consultant or designated expert witness, make sure the document examiner maintains competency in these tools and techniques.

Although the courts require expert witnesses to use a scientific approach, performing an examination of documents is rarely done in this manner. A pure scientific approach requires a double-blind experiment in which neither the person hiring the document examiner nor the document examiner are given information about the case.

A scientific approach is possible and desirable. It can be applied to a case by establishing a hypothesis then setting out to refute it. Each case is treated as a unique research project, the result of which is an opinion based strictly on the evidence provided to the document examiner. Ask your prospective examiner to describe how a scientific approach will be applied to your case.

Examination of handwriting may involve subjectivity. The National Academy of Sciences reported many forensic sciences, including handwriting examination, often are performed using an approach that is too subjective. Use of a repeatable methodology reduces the subjectivity of the examination. The document examiner can use quantitative methods when needed to improve the accuracy of the opinion. Quantitative methods include calculating proportional relationships among the zones of handwriting and measuring slant angles of characters. Use of software to overlay known and questioned writing allows the document examiner to provide the client with exhibits which demonstrate the reason for an opinion.

The document examiner must be aware of potential bias induced by knowing the client's desired results. The examiner is an advocate for the evidence itself, rather than the hiring attorney or the attorney's client. The focus of the work is determining whether the evidence supports the client's position.

Document examination involves more than examination of handwriting. Work is often performed to determine the type of printing used, whether a document has been altered, whether the document was constructed using computer techniques or if it is truly the document purported.

The document examiner you hire must have sufficient skill to examine more than the expected scope of work. Examination of handwriting may require analysis of the associated machine printing on the page, or determination whether the signature on the page is ink or was produced by a print process. A determination of the order in which overlapping signatures were placed onto the page may need to be performed.

Document examination is an investigative science. The required knowledge is rapidly changing due to proliferation of technology, computer generated documents and electronic signature pads. It takes skill, knowledge and experience for a document examiner to provide the highest degree of service to a client. Document examiners must attend sufficient training and education classes to maintain proficiency in the discipline.

A document examiner must be able to communicate with people not educated in the technical terminology of the field. Make sure the document examiner you hire is able to teach the trier of fact and the attorneys managing the case using common language and clear, demonstrative exhibits.

For questions about material in this book, contact Mike Wakshull at mikew@quality9.com. Your feedback is welcome.

Index

A

Altered Document. *See* Document, Altered

American Society of Questioned Document Examiners: 3

Angle of writing. *See* Writing, Angle of

ASTM: 11, 12, 14, 35, 60, 67, 73, 79, 83, 93

Attorney: 3, 23, 26, 27, 41, 77, 80, 81, 82, 85, 86, 90, 91, 92, 99

Authenticate: 6, 8

Authenticity: 1, 4, 6, 15, 16, 27, 41, 42, 88

Authenticity of Signature. *See* Signature, Authenticity of

B

Bias: 32, 60, 69, 75, 81, 82, 83, 84, 85, 86, 98, 113, 114

  Cognitive: 81, 83, 84

  Framing: 84, 85

Black's Law Dictionary: 3, 5, 8, 82, 113

Brain writing. *See* Writing, Brain

Legal: 25

Questioned: 8, 25, 27, 28, 35, 39, 51, 54, 61, 62, 64, 78, 86, 87, 116

Document examiner: 1, 2, 3, 4, 5, 6, 7, 8, 12, 14, 15, 19, 20, 21, 22, 23, 24, 25, 26, 27, 28, 33, 34, 35, 36, 37, 40, 41, 42, 43, 44, 46, 49, 50, 52, 53, 57, 58, 59, 60, 62, 64, 66, 67, 77, 78, 79, 80, 81, 82, 85, 86, 87, 88, 90, 91, 92, 93, 94, 95, 96, 97, 98, 99, 100, 116

E

Education requirements: 11, 93

Electrostatic detection device: 20

Eliminate: 6, 8, 14, 16, 63, 113

Errors: 82

  Grammatical: 82

  Typographical: 82

ESDA: 20

Ethics

  Code of: 3

Exemplars: 6, 15, 16, 23, 25, 26, 27, 39, 40, 41, 42, 62, 92

  Request: 25, 26, 27

Experience: 72, 78, 82, 93, 95, 97, 99

Expert: 2, 6, 10, 11, 63, 64, 70, 72, 73, 74, 75, 76, 77, 80, 81, 82, 83, 84, 85, 87, 93, 95, 97, 112

Expertise: 68, 70, 78, 112, 114

Intra-writer Variability. *See* Variability, Intra-writer

J

JPG: 61

Junk science: 10, 85

K

Kam: 64, 67, 68, 70, 71, 114

Known Document. *See* Document, Known

Known writing. *See* Writing, Known

Kumho Tire: 11, 76, 112

L

Laser Printer. *See* Printer, Laser

LaTrobe University: 12

Lead-in Stroke. *See* Stroke, Lead-in

Legal Document. *See* Document, Legal

Letter of Opinion. *See* Opinion, Letter of

Light

  Infrared: 17, 21, 44, 45, 49, 50

  Ultraviolet: 17, 21

Lindbergh baby kidnapping: 2

Line Sequence. *See* Sequence, Line

Lower zone. *See* Zone, Lower

Lupe: 18

T

U

Z

References

Ariely, D. (2008). Predictably irrational; The hidden forces that shape our decisions. New York, NY: Harper Perennial.

Arzy, S., Brezis, M., Khoury, S., Simon, S. & Ben-Hur, T. (2009). Misleading one detail: a preventable mode of diagnostic error? Journal of Evaluation in Clinical Practice, 15, 804-809.

Baer, M. A. (2005). Is an independent medical examination independent? The Forensic Examiner. Winter, 33.

Cialdini, R. (2001). Influence: science and practice. Boston: Allyn & Bacon.

Crisp. (2003). United States v. Crisp. 324 F.3d 261

Denbeaux, M. P., Risinger, M. D. (2003). Title: Kumho Tire and expert reliability: how the question you ask gives the answer you get Seaton Hall Law Review. 34(1), 15-75.

Dyer, A. G., Found, B & Rogers, D. (2006). Visual attention and expertise for forensic signature analysis. *Journal of Forensic Sciences*. 51(6), 1397 – 1404.

Eliot, T. S. (1943). *Little Gidding in Four Quartets.* Harcourt: San Diego.

Found, B. & Rogers, D. (2008). The probative character of forensic handwriting examiners' identification and elimination options on questioned signatures. *Forensic Science International.* 178, 54-60.

Freeman, F. N. (1914). *The teaching of handwriting.* Boston. Houghton Mifflin Company.

Garner, B. A. (editor) (2009). *Black's Law Dictionary Ninth Edition.* St. Paul: Thompson Reuters.

Giannelli, Paul C. "Confirmation bias in forensic testing." GP Solo 25.2 (2008): 22. General OneFile. Web. 13 Jan. 2010.

Harrison, W. (1981). *Suspect Documents, Their Scientific Examination.* Chicago: Nelson-Hall Publishers.

Hilton, O. (1995). The relationship of mathematical probability to the handwriting identification problem. *International Journal of Forensic Document Examiners.* (1 July/Sept)3, 224-229.

Hilton, O. (1993). *Scientific Examination of Documents Revised Edition.* Boca Raton, FL: CRC Press.

Huber, R. A. & Headrick, A. M. (1999). *Handwriting Identification: Facts and Fundamentals.* New York: CRC Press.

Kahneman, D., & Tversky, A. (1995). Conflict resolution: a cognitive perspective. In Arrow, K. et al. (Eds).

(1995) Barriers to conflict resolution. New York, NY: W.W. Norton & Company, Inc.

Kam, M., Weinstein, J. & Conn, R. (1994). Proficiency of professional document examiners in writer identification. *Journal of Forensic Sciences*, 39(1), 5-14.

McAlexander, T.V. (1999). Explaining qualified handwriting opinions to the jury. International Journal of Forensic Document *Examiners*. 5, 20-21.

McAuliff, B. D., Kovera, M. B. & Nunez, G. (2009). Can jurors recognize missing control groups, and experimenter bias in psychological science, Law and Human Behavior. 33, 247-257.

National Research Council (2009). *Strengthening forensic science in the United States: A path forward*. Washington, D.C. The National Academy Press.

Osborn, A. S. (1929). *Questioned Documents* (2nd Ed.). Albany, NY: Boyd Printing Company.

Risinger, M. J., Denbeaux, M. P. & Saks, M. D. (1989). Exorcism of ignorance as a proxy for rational knowledge: the lessons of handwriting identification "expertise". *University of Pennsylvania Law Review*. 137, 731-787.

Risinger, M. J. & Saks, M. D. (1996). Science and non-science in the courts: Daubert meets handwriting identification expertise. *Iowa Law Review*. 82(21), 1-52.

Srihari, S. N, Cha, S, Arora, H. & Lee, S. (2002). Individuality in handwriting. *Journal of Forensic Sciences*. 47(4),

1-17.

Schwab, A. P., (2008). Putting cognitive psychology to work: Improving decision-making in the medical encounter. Social Science & Medicine. 67, 1861-1869
Starzecpyzel, 1995. United States v. Starzecpyzel, 880 F. Supp. 1027 (S.D.N.Y. 1995).

Webber, S. (2008). The dark side of optimism; why looking on the bright side keeps us from thinking critically. The Conference Board Review. 45, 30-36.

About the Author

Mike Wakshull is a practicing civil and criminal court-qualified forensic document examiner based in Temecula, California. He partners with legal clients to dissect evidence presented in handwritten and computer-generated questioned documents.

His background includes founding a computer graphics software company and a project management consulting and training business. His work as a corporate trainer in information systems and project management took him to 4 continents. He managed global information systems policies and corporate quality risk management for a large biotechnology company. He applies skills from quality engineering, scientific training and information systems to document examination.

Wakshull served as chair of the 2012 National Association of Document Examiners conference and on the Board of Directors of the San Diego Chapter of Forensic Expert Witness Association. He has been an invited speaker at many national and international conferences. Wakshull was the only document examiner from the United States to speak at the World Congress of Forensics in China in October, 2011.

He holds a Master of Science degree in technology management from the University of Denver, a graduate school certificate in forensic document examination from East Tennessee State University and is a certified quality engineer.

Wakshull is on the adjunct faculty of the University of California at San Diego and Bellevue University.

.

Made in the USA
Charleston, SC
05 January 2013